# Whispers of the Heart

Sapphire Santiago

Copyright © 2024 by Sapphire Santiago
All rights reserved. No part of this publication may be
reproduced, stored or transmitted in any form or by any means, electronic, mechanical,
photocopying, recording, scanning, or otherwise without written permission from the
publisher. It is illegal to copy this book, post it to a website, or distribute it by any other means
without permission. This novel is entirely a work of fiction. The names, characters and incidents
portrayed in it are the work of the author's imagination. Any resemblance to actual persons,
living or dead, events or localities is entirely coincidental. Sapphire Santiago asserts the moral
right to be identified as the author of this work.

Designations used by companies to distinguish their products
are often claimed as trademarks. All brand names and product
names used in this book and on its cover are trade names,
service marks, trademarks and registered trademarks of their
respective owners. The publishers and the book are not
associated with any product or vendor mentioned in this book.
None of the companies referenced within the book have endorsed the book.

First edition

Contents
**Dedication**

**I Love**
1 Yearning for Love
2 Affection
3 Soft Spot
4 Appreciation
5 Adore
6 Savor
7 Committed
8 Love Languages
9 My World
10 Cherish
11 Embrace
12 Change

**II Self-love**
13 Beautiful
14 Fly
15 Talk
16 New Rules
17 Miss Me
18 Found
19 Loved
20 Now and Then
21 Eyes
22 Self-love
23 Hobbies
24 Moon

**III Friendship**
25 Friendship
26 Bond
27 Closer
28 Platonic Soulmate

29 Forever
30 Trust
31 Unconditional Love
32 True Friend
33 Accepting
34 Honest
35 Important
36 Positive

**IV Heartbreak**
37 When Will I Be the First Option?
38 Love is Hard
39 Heartbreak
40 Reality
41 Trauma
42 Longing
43 Suffering
44 Pain/Hurt
45 Deep Longing
46 Lost Love
47 Influenced
48 Rejected
49 Denial

**V Mental Health**
50 As I Look Up Into the Sky
51 Escape
52 Value
53 Mental Health
54 Piece of Me
55 Take Care of Yourself
56 BrOKen
57 Mystery
58 Awareness
59 Improve
60 Shield
61 Relax

**Acknowledgements**

# Dedication

*This is a sign to follow your heart.*

*Love*

## Yearning for Love

In a world of fleeting glances,
She longs for timeless romances.
Hand in hand, beneath moonlight's gleam,
Her heart seeks love from a bygone dream.
In fields of roses, she yearns to stroll,
With a love that fills her soul.
Whispers shared in ancient tongues,
Echoing melodies from love's young lungs.
Through cobbled streets, they'd aimlessly roam,
Finding solace in each other's home.
In quaint cafes, their laughter would chime,
Lost in a love that withstands time.
But in a modern world, she finds,
Love's essence seems confined.
Yet still, she dreams of days of yore,
Where love was simple, forevermore.

# Affection

In whispers soft and twilight's glow,
Affection blooms and starts to grow,
A gentle touch, a kindred gaze,
In love's sweet dance
our hearts engage.
Through every word, in every deed,
It's more than want, it's what we need,
A bond that time cannot erase,
Affection's warmth, a tender's grace.
In laughter's lilt and tear's caress,
It's there to soothe, to comfort, bless
A silent pact between two souls,
Together strong, together whole.
So let it flow, let it shine,
This gift of love, forever thine
In every hug, in every kiss,
Affection is eternal bliss.

# Appreciation

In a world of hustle and haste,
Let's take a moment, no time to waste.
To appreciate the simple things,
The joy that each new day brings.
For in the chaos, there's beauty found,
In every sight, in every sound.
The warmth of sunlight on our face,
The melody of laughter's embrace.
Appreciation, like a gentle breeze,
Fills our hearts with a sense of ease.
It shines a light on what's truly dear,
Reminding us to hold it near.
So let's be grateful, my dear friend,
For the love and support on which we can depend.
For the moments both big and small,
That make life worth cherishing, overall.
Appreciation, a gift so grand,
Let's spread it across the land.
For in gratitude, we truly see,
The beauty of life's tapestry

# Adore

In whispers of the dawn, so pure,
A tale of fondness, sweet and sure.
Beneath the sky's vast, azure floor,
Lies the heart's quiet, gentle roar.
Adore, they say, is soft and kind,
A dance of souls, with stars aligned.
In every beat, in every mind,
It's love's own treasure that we find.
With every glance, a flame ignites,
Through day's bright laughs and velvet nights.
In every touch, the spirit alights,
Adore, the warmth that heart invites.
It's in the laughter of a child,
In every nature's creature wild.
In every garden, undefiled,
Adore lives on, forever mild.
So let us cherish this embrace,
And in our hearts, give it a space.
For adore, with its tender grace,
Makes this world a better place

# Savor

In the realm of love, let's savor each touch,
A symphony of emotions that means so much.
Like a sweet melody, love dances in the air,
In every moment, a treasure to share.
Savor the tenderness of a gentle caress,
The warmth of a hug, a love that's boundless.
In every kiss, a taste of pure bliss,
A connection so deep, we can't resist.
Savor the laughter that love brings,
The joy and happiness that make our hearts sing.
In every smile, a glimpse of pure delight,
A love that shines through both day and night.
Savor the moments, big and small,
The shared experiences that make us feel tall.
In every memory, a love that's true,
A bond that grows stronger with me and you.
So let's savor love, my dear friend,
In its embrace, let our hearts mend.
For in the sweetness of our embrace,
We find a love that time can't erase.

# Love Languages

Whispers of affection in acts so kind,
Love Languages that we each find.
Words of affirmation, softly spoken,
In every compliment, love's token.
Quality time, a precious gift,
In shared moments, spirits lift.
Undivided attention, presence so true,
In the here and now, just me and you.
Acts of service, deeds that show,
In the giving, love does grow.
Easing burdens, a helping hand,
In every chore, love takes a stand.
Gifts that speak from the heart,
Tokens of love, a work of art.
Wrapped in thoughtfulness, tied with care,
In every present, love's there to share.
Physical touch, a tender embrace,
In every hug, a loving space.
A kiss, a cuddle, warmth to impart,
In every touch, a language of the heart.
Love Languages, unique and diverse,
In every dialect, our love converses.

Understanding yours and mine,
In love's dialogue, we intertwine.

# Committed

Committed to the path that we both tread,
A journey of hearts, where love has led.
With every step, a promise kept,
In love's warm hold, we've both leapt.
Committed to dreams we dare to chase.
With trust as our compass, we create.
Committed to laughter, to tears, to growth,
To the silent vows, we both swore an oath.
In the tapestry of time, our threads entwine,
With every fiber, your heart meets mine.
Committed to you, in every way,
My love, my light, my night and day.
In every beat, my heart confesses,
A love committed, it caresses.

## My World

In my world, you're the morning sun,
Rising high when the day's begun.
You're the laughter in every breeze,
The quiet strength in towering trees.
In my world, you're the evening star,
Guiding light from realms afar.
You're the comfort of the night,
In darkness, you're my brightest light.
In my world, you're the gentle rain,
Easing heartache, soothing pain.
You're the rainbow's vibrant hue,
A promise that every word is true.
In my world, you're the mountain's might,
Standing firm with all your height.
You're the ocean's endless song,
In your rhythm, I belong.
In my world, you're all that's good,
The peace and joy of my neighborhood.
You're every hope that I hold dear,
With you close, I've nothing to fear.

# Cherish

Cherish this fleeting, precious time,
A rhythm felt, a silent chime.
In every heartbeat, in every breath,
A dance with life, a waltz with death.
Hold dear the love that you receive,
The bonds you forge, the webs you weave.
In every smile, a story told,
In every hand, there's warmth to hold.
Cherish the sunset painted skies,
The whispers of the wind's soft sighs.
In nature's arms, we find our peace,
In her embrace, our worries cease.
Embrace the now, the here, the you,
For moments pass like morning dew.
Cherish the journey, not the race,
In every step, find your grace.
Let's cherish memories, old and new,
They're the light guiding us through.
A treasure chest of times so dear,
Cherish them all, year to year.

## Soft Spot

In hidden corners of the heart,
A soft spot lives, set apart,
A tender nook, a secret space,
Where warmth and fondness interlace.
It's there in smiles that reach the eyes,
In gentle words that emphasize,
A sanctuary from life's rough thought,
Each soul's sweet, vulnerable soft spot.
It thrives in memories held dear,
In moments when loved ones are near,
A cushion for the times we're not,
This precious, loving spot.
Embrace it in its quiet might,
Let it guide you through the night,
For when the world feels cold and fraught,
Seek refuge in your soft spot

## Embrace

In the warmth of an embrace, we find solace,
A tender moment, where hearts interlace.
In arms outstretched, worries fade away,
As love and comfort have the final say.
Embrace the laughter, the joy it brings,
The melody that in our hearts sings.
Hold tight to moments, both big and small,
For in their embrace, we find our all.
Embrace the challenges that come our way,
For they shape us, help us grow each day.
With courage and strength, we'll rise above,
Embracing the journey, with endless love.
So let us embrace life's ebb and flow,
With open hearts and let love's river flow.
In each other's arms, we'll always find,
A place of solace, a love that's kind.
Embrace this moment, let worries release,
For in each embrace, we find inner peace.

# Change

Change is swift, love adapts,
Together they dance, no time elapsed.
Hearts in flux, but still they cling,
Through every shift, love's bell rings.

*Self-love*

## New Rules

New Rules for a life so true,
Penned with the ink of self-love's hue.
Rule one, be kind within your mind,
In gentle thoughts, your worth you'll find.
Rule two, let go of past mistakes,
Each step you take, self-love awakes.
Rule three, embrace the you today,
In self-love's light, you'll find your way.
New Rules to live, to love, to be,
In self-love's book, you hold the key.
With every rule, you'll start to see,
Self-love's the path to being free.

## Beautiful

In the mirror, a story untold,
Self-love's tale, brave and bold.
Beauty's within, not just skin-deep,
In self-love's embrace, confidence we reap.
Beautiful mind, beautiful soul,
Loving yourself, the ultimate goal.
In every flaw, perfection's seed,
Self-love is the most beautiful deed.
Embrace your quirks, your unique light,
In self-acceptance, you shine so bright.
Beautiful you, in all your ways,
In self-love's glow, you'll spend your days.

# Fly

Spread your wings, it's time to soar,
Self-love's the wind, it's at your core.
Fly above doubts, fears, and lies,
In self-love's sky, your spirit flies.
Fly to heights where dreams are clear,
Where love for self dispels all fear.
On self-love's breeze, you'll find your way,
Fly free, for you are here to stay.

## Talk

Let's have a talk, just me and you,
About self-love and all it can do.
Speak kind words, let the negative depart,
With every self-talk, heal your heart.
Talk up your strengths, embrace every part,
Self-love's language is a beautiful art.
In the chat with yourself, be your own friend,
For self-love's talk should uplift, not offend.

## Miss Me

Miss me with a twist so sweet,
Self-love's journey, no small feat.
Miss the days of self-doubt and fear,
For now, in love with self, you're here.
Miss me not, for I'm still near,
In every moment, self-love's cheer.
With every step, I've found my grace,
In self-love's mirror, I see my face.

# Found

In the quest of self, I sought,
Through battles fought and lessons taught.
In the maze of mind, I wandered, bound,
Till in the depths, self-love was found.
Found a peace within my soul,
Self-love's touch has made me whole.
In the mirror, a new friend's face,
With self-love, I've found my place.
No longer lost, no longer blind,
In self-love's arms, myself I find.
A treasure that was always there,
Found at last, beyond compare.

# Loved

Loved, not by another's grace,
But from the heart in my own space.
Self-love's the whisper in the breeze,
The warm embrace in the rustling trees.
Loved by me, myself, and I,
Beneath the vast, unending sky.
No longer seeking to be proved,
For in my soul, I have truly bloomed.
Self-love's the song that's softly sung,
In every verse, my spirit sprung.
Loved for all that I am within,
With self-love, life's a joyful spin.

# Now and Then

Now and Then, a tale unfolds,
Of self-love's journey, brave and bold.
Then was doubt, a silent scream,
Now is love, a waking dream.
Then I searched for worth outside,
Now within, I take my stride.
Self-love's seed, once sown so thin,
Now blooms forth from deep within.
Then echoed others' harsh critiques,
Now my heart to self-love speaks.
From then to now, the change begins,
Self-love's light, from within, it wins.

# Eyes

Eyes that see beyond the skin,
Finding love for self within.
Gazing deep, where truth does dwell,
Self-love's story, they do tell.
Eyes that sparkle with self-kindness,
Reflecting growth, not inner blindness.
In their light, no shadows cast,
For self-love's vision holds me fast.
Through these eyes, I now perceive,
The love I give, the love I receive.
Eyes of self-love, clear and true,
Showing me all I can do.

# Self-love

Self-love, a gentle inner glow,
A steady flame that comes to grow.
Nurtured by the kindest deeds,
It blossoms, meeting all one's needs.
A whisper in the quiet night,
A dawn that breaks with softest light.
Self-love, the root of inner peace,
Where harsh judgments finds release.
In self-love's soil, confidence blooms,
Dispelling all the inner glooms.
A journey inward, to the core,
Where self-love opens every door.

# Friendship

# Friendship

Friendship, a bond that's true,
A treasure chest for me and you.
Shared laughter, secrets kept,
In friendship's fold, we've all wept.
Together strong, together kind,
In each other, strength we find.
A journey shared, a path so bright,
Friendship's flame burns ever light.

## Bond

Bond, unspoken, yet understood,
Stronger than oak, more lasting than wood.
In smiles and tears, a silent pact,
In friendship's bond, our hearts react.
Side by side, or miles apart,
This bond endures, a work of art.
A thread that weaves through time and space,
In every bond, friendship cannot be replaced.

## Closer

Closer, with each shared tale,
Friendship's ship sets hearty sail.
Laughter, whispers, trust, and care,
In friendship's dance, a perfect pair.
Through storms and calm, we navigate,
Closer still, we resonate.
In every joy, in every sorrow,
Friendship promises a brighter tomorrow.

# Platonic Soulmate

Platonic Soulmate, hearts align,
Beyond the stars, your spirit's mine.
In laughter's echo, whispers shared,
A bond so deep, nothing compared.
No romance sought, yet love abounds,
In every beat, friendship resounds.
Souls in sync, a perfect duet,
A friendship that I'll never forget.

## Forever

Forever, a promise in the wind,
In the heart of friendship, we're akin.
Through changing seasons, come what may,
Our bond endures, day by day.
In silent moments, loud with care,
In every memory, we're there.
Forever not just a length of time,
But depth of bond, in friendship's prime.

# Trust

Trust, the anchor of our ties,
In the vault of friendship, it never dies.
A silent language, hearts converse,
In trust, our fears we disperse.
Hand in hand, or miles away,
Trust in friendship, come what may.
The unseen glue that holds us fast,
In the realm of trust, friendship lasts.

## Unconditional Love

Unconditional Love, without a clause,
In friendship's realm, it gives us pause.
No terms set, no scores to keep,
In this love, the roots run deep.
Through storms and calm, it stays so true,
A friendship's love, forever new.
No judgment cast, no end, no start,
Unconditional love, the heart of the heart.

## True Friend

True Friend, a beacon ever bright,
Guiding through the darkest night.
A heart that listens, understands,
A bond that's crafted with gentle hands.
In laughter and in tears the same,
A true friend's love remains aflame.
Through every trial, this bond we mend,
In you, I've found a true friend.

## Accepting

Accepting, a harbor safe and sound,
Where friendship's truest joys are found.
Differences embraced with open arms,
In acceptance, we find no alarms.
With every flaw, we build our trust,
Accepting each other, because we must.
In the warmth of this gentle embrace,
Friendship thrives in such a space.

# Honest

Honesty, a rare, pure gold,
In friendship's heart, it takes its hold.
No shadows cast, no veils to hide,
In honesty, friends like to confide.
Words sincere, like stars at night,
Guide us with their gentle light.
In every truth, our trust we find,
Honesty, the strongest bind.

# Important

Important, the whispers in the breeze,
The strength we find on bended knees.
In every moment, friendship's light,
Turns looming darkness into bright.
The silent rock, the laughter's tune,
Under sunlit skies or crescent moon.
In life's vast canvas, stroke by stroke,
Friendship's the art, the heart's bespoke.

*Heartbreak*

# When Will I Be the First Option?

In the shadows, I linger unseen,
Watching you chase after dreams.
Am I but a shadow, a mere distraction,
In your world of endless attraction?
When will I be the first option?
Not just a passing notion.
When will you see me, truly,
And not just as a beauty?
I've given my heart, my all,
Yet still, I feel so small.
Questioning every move I make,
Wondering if it's all a mistake.
When will I be the first option?
To have your love without caution.
To be cherished, to be adored,
Not just when you're feeling bored.
In this one-sided dance, I sway,
Hoping for a brighter day.
When will I be the one you choose,
And my love, you'll never lose?

# Heartbreak

Heartbreak, a somber, heavy tune,
Echoes in chambers emptied too soon.
Love's vibrant colors fade to grey,
As whispered promises drift away.
Tender bonds, once firm and sure,
Fracture beneath doubts that endure.
The heart, a canvas torn to pieces,
Bears the scars of a love that no decreases.
Gone the laughter, the shared dreams of night,
Only shadows remain, bereft of light.
Yet through the pain, the soul learns to cope,
For even in heartbreak, there lies hope.

# Reality

Reality, a stark and truthful sting,
Where heartbreak's bell solemnly rings.
Love's sweet mirage, now clear in sight,
Reveals the end of a once-bright flight.
In this realm, true colors show,
And what's left is the afterglow.
A heart once whole, now split in two,
Accepting what's gone, embracing the new.
The dreams we held, now touch the ground,
A sobering fall, without a sound.
Yet in this reality, we find our might,
To rise once more, into the light.

# Trauma

Trauma, the echo of love's demise,
A silent scream that never dies.
It lingers in the hollow space,
Where once was warmth, now cold embrace.
The heart, it beats, yet feels so numb,
Replaying the tune that can't be undone.
Shards of trust, scattered wide,
In the wake of where love did once reside.
A ghostly dance of what was pure,
Now a haunting refrain, ever obscure.
With each throb, the soul does yearn,
For the tender touch of love's return.

# Longing

Longing, a whisper in the heart's deep well,
A yearning for what time cannot dispel.
The echo of a touch, a glance, a kiss,
In heartbreak's shadow, it's you I miss.
The empty chair, the silent phone,
A text unsent, the nights alone.
A chasm wide, where love once lay,
Longing for you, every single day.
The laughter shared, now a quiet space,
Memories linger, I can't erase.
A hopeful gaze towards the door,
Longing for a love that is no more.

## Suffering

Suffering, the constant ache within,
A silent battle no one can win.
The remnants of a love now lost,
Heartbreak's frost, the bitter cost.
Each beat, a reminder of the past,
A love once vibrant, not meant to last.
Suffering in the quiet of the night,
Where shadows dwell and out of sight.
A soul searching for its missing part,
A puzzle undone, right from the start.
Enduring the pain, the endless fight,
Suffering alone, without respite.

# Pain

Pain, a relentless, unseen force,
A heartbreak's path, a turbulent course.
The sting of love that's slipped away,
Hurt that grips and holds its sway.
A silent tear, a hidden scar,
The ache of wishing from afar.
Love's sweet bloom now wilted, spent,
Pain, the cost of love's lament.
In the quiet hurt, we search for why,
Underneath the vast, indifferent sky.
Yet through the hurt, we slowly learn,
To rise, to heal, to love in turn.

# Deep Longing

Deep Longing, an endless, silent call,
A heart that aches, a tear that falls.
The void where once two souls did cling,
Now echoes with the pain of deep longing.
Nights stretch on, a canvas of despair,
Painted with memories of a love so rare.
Whispers of the past, a haunting song,
For the one who's gone, where they belong.
In dreams, I reach, but you fade away,
A cruel mirage by the light of day.
Deep longing, a love that can't be wrong,
A heart that waits, forever long.

# Lost Love

Lost Love, a tale too often told,
A flame that burns until it's cold.
The embers of a once fierce fire,
Now smoldering in the pyre.
Gone the warmth, the laughter light,
Leaving shadows in its flight.
A void where once did beat a heart,
Now torn and silent, ripped apart.
Lost Love, the cruelest thief,
Steals the night, a haunting grief.
In the stillness, echoes call,
Of the love that was my all.

# Influenced

Influenced by whispers of the past,
A heart that loved, not meant to last.
Echoes of words, once sweetly spoken,
Now leave that same heart bruised and broken.
Promises swayed by the softest breeze,
Turned to dust, lost with ease.
Influenced by a love so bright,
Now dims the stars once in my sight.
A dance to a tune that fades away,
Leaves the heart in disarray.
Influenced to leap, to trust, to fall,
Heartbreak, the cruelest master of all.

# Rejected

Rejected, a silent scream within,
A door closed, where love can't begin.
The sting of hope that's swiftly dashed,
A tender heart, scornfully slashed.
Words unmet with warm embrace,
Turn away, hide the face.
Rejected dreams, like leaves in the wind,
Scattered far, where longing had been.
A hollow echo in the chest,
Where once beat love, now unrest.
In the quiet aftermath of the break,
Lies the heavy toll of heartache.

# Denial

Denial, a shield, a lie's embrace,
Hides the heartache I can't face.
A smile worn, while inside I weep,
Love lost, a wound too deep.

## Love is Hard

Love is hard
The one that you wish for
Simply doesn't exist anymore
You're exhausted
Saying the same thing over and over
All you want to do is wish on a four-leaf clover

Mentally tired
Physically tired
Emotionally tired
Love is hard

Why must this generation be difficult
All I want is someone significant
I want someone who will TRY
I want someone who WILL CARE
Just so I don't have to cry
Just so I don't have to declare
The words
No more

Mentally tired

Physically tired
Emotionally tired
Love is hard

*Mental Health*

# As I Look Up Into the Sky

As I look up into the sky
Sometimes I wonder why,
The good get hurt
And the bad get dessert.
We keep a smile on our face
No matter the harm,
But when we get back to our place
We try to stay calm.
As I look up into the sky
Sometimes I wonder why,
The good get damaged
And the bad managed.

## Escape

Escape into a tranquil sea,
A mind in search of harmony.
Waves of thought begin to ease,
As breath and calm restore the peace.
A mental maze, once dark and deep,
Now finds the light, awakes from sleep.
Escape the chains of silent strife,
To sail towards a healthier life.

# Value

Value, not in silver or in gold,
But in the stories yet untold.
The worth within, often unseen,
In every breath, where we've been.
Mental health, a hidden gem,
Treasured more than any diadem.
Nurture it with gentle care,
For its value is beyond compare.

## Mental Health

Mental health, a silent stream,
Flowing through life's grand scheme.
A force unseen but deeply felt,
In its presence, hearts do melt.
A journey through the mind's vast space,
Seeking solace, a tender grace.
It shapes our days, our dreams at night,
In its balance, we find our light.

# Piece of Me

Piece of me, a fragment shared,
With mental health, so deeply paired.
A puzzle piece, unique and true,
Reflects the struggles we push through.
In every thought, a piece of soul,
Seeking peace to make us whole.
Mental health, the cornerstone,
In this journey, we're not alone.

## Take Care of Yourself

Take care of yourself, a gentle plea,
To tend the mind like a precious tree.
Nourish the roots, embrace the self,
For mental health is truest wealth.
In self-care, find strength anew,
In every breath, let love shine through.
Heed the call, your needs to tend,
For in your health, the heart will mend.

# BrOKen

BrOKen, yet in every crack, light,
Creeping in to banish night.
In fractured spaces, courage dwells,
A story only bravery tells.
Mental health, not always seen,
But felt in spaces in between.
In brokenness, we find our might,
In every dawn after the night.

# Mystery

Mystery, a shrouded lane,
Where thoughts like shadows, ebb and wane.
The mind—a labyrinth, vast, profound,
Where many a secret can be found.
With mental health, the paths we tread,
Are often twisted, filled with dread.
Yet through the maze, we seek the light,
To understand our inner fight.

## Awareness

Awareness, a beacon bright,
In the silent struggle, a guiding light.
It whispers softly, "You're not alone,"
In the mind's vast, uncharted zone.
With open eyes, we start to see,
The chains of stigma we can free.
Awareness blooms, and with each petal,
A step towards the middle ground we settle.

## Improve

Improve, a journey day by day,
A path where healing finds its way.
With every step, the mind grows strong,
In self-care's tune, life's sweetest song.
Mind's garden, tended with grace,
Blooms with progress in its embrace.
Each petal, a victory small,
In mental health, the growth of all.

# Shield

Shield, a guard in the mind's great hall,
A protector standing firm and tall.
Against the waves of doubt and fear,
It stands to hold your well-being near.
With strength, it wards off anxious thoughts,
A battle daily, bravely fought.
In mental health, this shield's embrace,
Safeguards the heart, a tranquil space.

## Relax

Relax, breathe in peace, let go,
Ease the mind, let calmness flow.

## Acknowledgements

Thank you to my family for supporting me throughout my journey and encouraging me to never give up on my dreams.

Thank you to my best friends! Without them, these poems will never be alive!

Thank you to YOU GUYS, the readers for reading this book and adding it to your collection! Let's hope you can add even more of my books to your collection!

Made in the USA
Columbia, SC
28 October 2024